How to Knit

Slip knot

This will keep the yarn on your needles and also form your first stitch.

1. Make a loop at the end of your yarn.

2. Create a new loop in the yarn and pull it through, as shown.

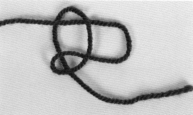

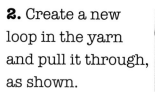

3. Carefully slip the end of one needle through the loop.

4. Pull both ends of the yarn tight to secure the knot on the needle.

Casting on

Follow these easy steps to cast on your yarn.

1. Wrap the yarn over and around your thumb, as shown.

2. Place the needle through the yarn.

3. Pull the yarn off your thumb and onto the needle. Pull to tighten.

4. Cast on the number of stitches as shown on row one of your template.

Knit stitch

When you are starting a new row, hold the needle with the stitches in your left hand. Knit from right to left, holding the yarn in your right hand.

3a. From above, the yarn has created a loop around each needle, as shown.

3b. Insert the right-hand needle into the front of the left-hand loop, crossing the left-hand needle.

1. Push the right-hand needle under the first stitch so the needles are crossed.

4. Pull the right-hand needle and loop off the left-hand needle. Pull the stitch tight.

2. Wrap the yarn around the right-hand needle counterclockwise (from back to front). It should lie between the two needles.

5. When you have finished a row, count the stitches to make sure you haven't dropped any. Now hold this needle in your left hand.

Projects by Bethany Hines

Licensed exclusively to Top That Publishing Ltd
Tide Mill Way, Woodbridge, Suffolk, IP12 1AP, UK
www.topthatpublishing.com
Copyright © 2016 Tide Mill Media
0 2 4 6 8 9 7 5 3 1
Manufactured in Zhejiang, China

Getting Started

Knitting is one of the coolest crafts around, and what could be "cooler" than making a collection of knitted winter critters? When you've mastered the basic techniques explained on the next few pages, you'll be ready to start making the cutest knitted animals ever!

Before you begin...

It's a good idea to gather together all your knitting equipment and materials before you begin, so look at the list of things you'll need at the start of each project. In addition to the knitting needles supplied, you'll need a sewing needle, a yarn needle, scissors, pins, fabric glue, a pencil, and tracing paper. You'll also need a selection of craft materials including colored yarn, colored felt, stuffing, embroidery thread, and decorations such as sequins, beads, and buttons. You can find all of these things in craft or hobby stores, or you can buy them online.

Using templates

The projects have templates and liners for you to use. Once you're confident at knitting, you could always adapt these, and the colors of your cool creatures, to make your own creations!

Adult help required!

While you're learning the basics of knitting, ask an adult to help you. You'll be knitting solo in no time!

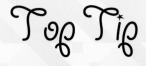

Top Tip

Keep your equipment, materials, and knitting projects safely in one place, such as an old cake tin or a knitting bag. The easier it is to carry around, the better!

 WARNING!

Take care when using knitting needles, sewing needles, and scissors, as they have sharp points.

Increasing

Add an extra stitch to a row to increase your knitting.

1. Knit one stitch as normal, but don't pull it off the left-hand needle.

2. Pull the right-hand needle behind the left-hand needle, as shown.

3. Push the right-hand needle into the back of the stitch on the left-hand needle, as shown.

4. Wrap the yarn counterclockwise around the right-hand needle. Knit the stitch off as normal, pulling it off the left-hand needle.

5. You should now have two stitches on your right-hand needle.

Decreasing

Remove stitches from a row to decrease the size of your knitting.

1. Push the right-hand needle through the first two stitches on the left-hand needle.

2. Wrap the yarn counterclockwise around the right-hand needle and down through the middle.

3. Pull the right-hand needle under the stitches and to the front of the left-hand needle.

4. Pull the stitches off the left-hand needle. You should have one stitch on the right-hand needle.

Casting off

Take the stitches off the needle one by one.

1. Knit two stitches.

2. Use the left-hand needle to lift the first stitch over the second stitch and off the tip of the needles.

3. Knit another stitch as normal. Again use the left-hand needle to pull the first stitch over the second and off the needles.

4. Repeat step 3 until only one stitch is on the right-hand needle.

5. Loosen the stitch and pull out the needle.

6. Cut the yarn off the ball (leave about 4 in.) and thread the end back through the loop. Pull the thread tight to secure.

Dropped stitch

If you spot a hole in your work, you have probably dropped a stitch.

1. Knit to the end of the row. Carefully slide the knitting needle out of the stitches.

2. Gently pull the yarn, so the rows unravel to the row where you dropped the stitch. Make sure you unravel this row too.

3. Carefully push the left-hand needle through the stitches again, making sure you catch all of them, including the dropped stitch. Count to make sure! Now carry on knitting.

Sewing in ends

When your knitting is finished you can neaten it by sewing in loose ends.

1. Thread an end onto an embroidery needle.

2. Push the needle through the edge of the knitting, about five or six rows.

3. Pull the yarn through, then trim the end. Repeat with the other loose end.

Sewing up seams

Sew up pieces of knitting to create larger pieces or shapes.

1. Take a new piece of yarn and thread it onto an embroidery needle.

2. Hold the two pieces of knitting together and use running stitch to sew along the seams to hold them together.

3. When you have sewn the whole seam, cut the yarn and use the needle to tuck both ends back into the knitting.

Running stitch

Tie a knot at the end of your thread or yarn. Push the needle into the fabric, or knitting, and back out again. Repeat until you have completed your sewing, then finish with a knot.

Templates

Follow the templates to knit the pieces for each project.

Rows ● = one stitch

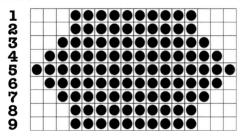

1. To use the template, count the number of stitches in row one. Always start at the top of the grid.

2. Cast this number of stitches onto your needle.

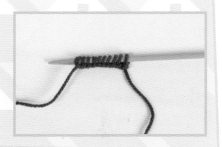

3. Count the number of stitches in row two. This is the number of stitches you need for your second row of knitting.

4. Increase or decrease the number of stitches for each row, as shown on the template.

Knitted Narwhal

Narwhal whales live in the Arctic and are famous for having an amazing tusk.

You will need:

- yarn in blue and white • knitting needles
- pins • needle and thread
- stuffing • a pipe cleaner
- scissors • fabric glue
- two buttons, or black felt

1. First, use the body template opposite to knit two body pieces in the blue yarn.

2. Then, use the fins template to knit two fins in the same color yarn as the body.

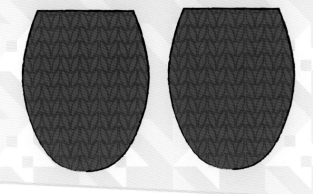

3. Lay the two body pieces on top of each other. Place the straight ends of each fin between the body pieces, about halfway down. Pin all of the layers together.

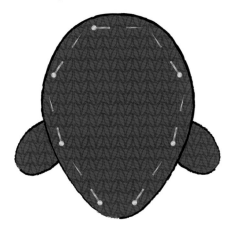

Cool Fact

A narwhal's "tusk" is actually one of its canine teeth!

4. Sew along the edge of the body pieces to secure the fins, as shown. Leave a small gap at the bottom where you can add stuffing.

5. Push stuffing into the narwhal's body, making sure you push it up to the top with your fingers. When the body is full enough, sew up the hole at the bottom.

6. Using the tail template, knit a tail for your narwhal in the same color yarn that you used to make the body and fins.

7. Place the tail at the back of the narwhal and sew into place with a few large stitches.

Templates

Each dot represents the number of stitches on each row.

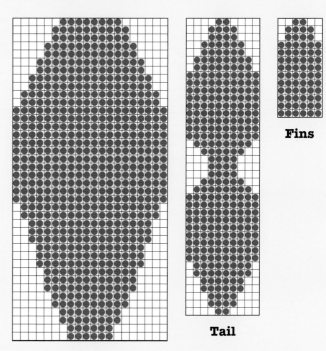

Fins

Tail

Body

8. Ask an adult to cut the pipe cleaner so that it measures roughly 2¼ in. long.

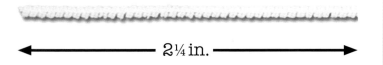

← ——— 2¼ in. ——— →

9. Push the pipe cleaner into the front of the narwhal where you want the tusk to be. Make sure you push it far enough so that it is held in place.

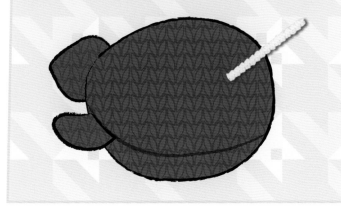

10. Wrap white yarn around the pipe cleaner, starting at the base. Wrap more layers around the base and fewer at the tip, making a cone shape, as shown. Thread the yarn at the tip onto an embroidery needle and poke it down through the tusk, then out near the base, and trim the end. Do the same with the loose yarn at the base, poking it into the body.

11. Glue on black felt circles for the eyes, or stitch on buttons if you prefer.

12. Using white yarn, sew on a smile shape in small, neat stitches. Sew in any loose ends of yarn to complete.

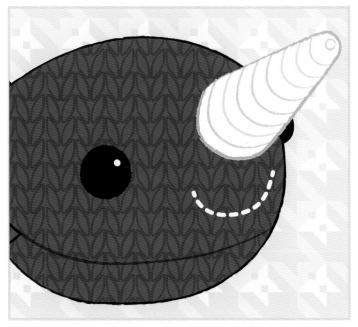

Top Tip

Use a variety of blue and gray yarns to make a whole family of cute narwhals!

Knitted Snowy Owl

Follow these steps to make your own cuddly snowy owl!

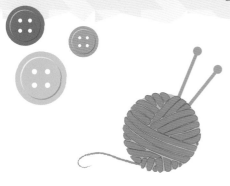

You will need:

- light-colored yarn • knitting needles
- tracing paper • felt or patterned fabric
- pins • needle and thread • stuffing
- scissors • fabric glue
- two buttons, or black felt

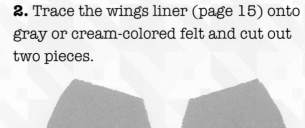

2. Trace the wings liner (page 15) onto gray or cream-colored felt and cut out two pieces.

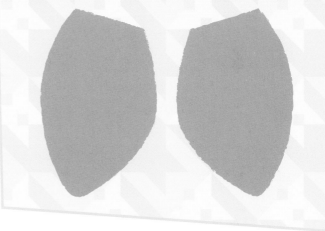

3. Lay the two body pieces on top of each other. Place the straight ends of each wing between the body pieces, about halfway down, as shown. Pin all of the layers together.

1. First, use the body template (page 15) to knit two body pieces in the color you want your owl to be. Snowy owls' feathers turn lighter as they get older.

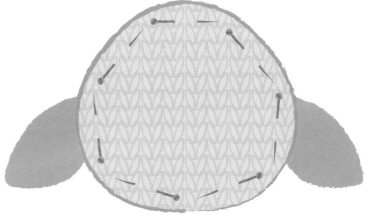

4. Sew along the edge of the body pieces to secure the wings, as shown. Leave a small gap at the bottom where you can add stuffing.

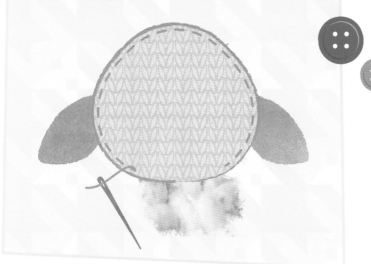

5. Push stuffing into the owl's body, making sure you push it up to the top with your fingers. When the body is full enough, sew up the hole at the bottom.

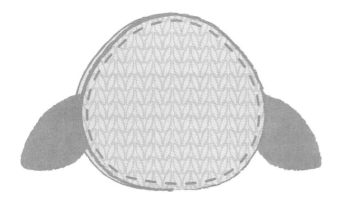

6. Use the ears template to knit two ears in the same color yarn that you used for the body.

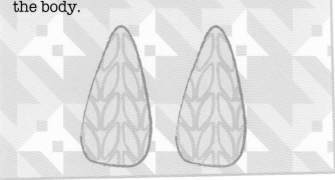

7. Sew the ears onto either side of the owl's head, as shown.

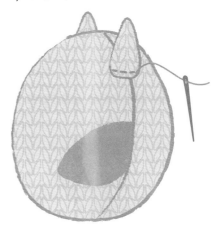

8. Trace the feet liner onto orange felt and cut out two pieces. Glue these into place on the bottom of the owl.

9. Trace the outer eyes liner onto the same color felt you used for the wings and cut two pieces. Glue in place, as shown.

10. For the inner eyes, glue on black felt circles, or stitch on buttons if you prefer.

11. Trace the beak liner onto orange felt and cut out the shape. Place it onto the owl's face and stitch through the center to hold in place. Sew in any loose ends of yarn to complete.

Top Tip

Why not try making the wings, feet, and outer eyes from different-colored felts.

Templates

Each dot represents the number of stitches on each row.

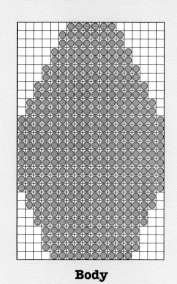

Body

Ears

Liners

Liners are to scale.

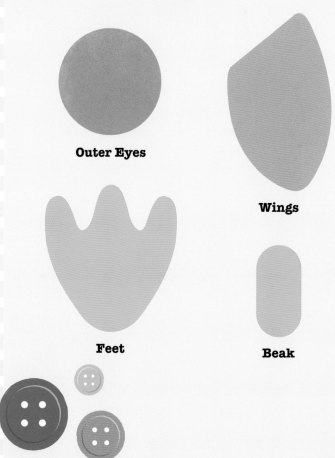

Outer Eyes

Wings

Feet

Beak

Knitted Polar Bear

Can you help give this adorable polar bear a good home?

You will need:

- yarn in white and a color of your choice
- knitting needles • tracing paper
- felt or patterned fabric • pins
- needle and thread • stuffing • scissors
- fabric glue • three buttons, or black felt

1. Use the polar bear body template opposite to knit two body pieces in white yarn.

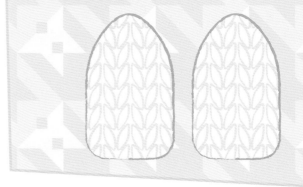

2. Use the ears template to knit two ears using white yarn.

3. Trace the ears liner onto pink felt and cut out two pieces. Glue the ear liners on top of each knitted ear and place to one side.

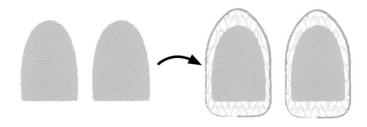

4. Use the arms template to knit two arms in white yarn. Fold each arm in half and stitch along the edge, as shown. Place to one side.

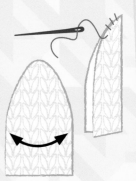

5. Use the feet template to knit two white feet. Fold each foot in half and stitch around the edge leaving a gap at the bottom. Fill each foot with stuffing.

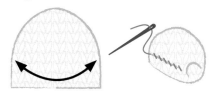

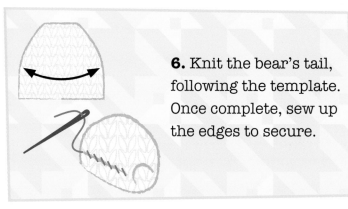

6. Knit the bear's tail, following the template. Once complete, sew up the edges to secure.

7. Lay the two body pieces on top of each other, as shown, and pin together. Then sew along the edge, joining the pieces together. Leave a small gap at the bottom where you can add stuffing.

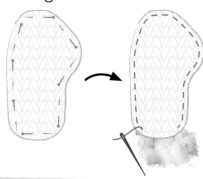

8. Push stuffing into the body, making sure you push it up to the top with your fingers. When the body is half full, tightly tie a piece of matching yarn around the middle of the body to make the head, then trim the ends.

Templates

Each dot represents the number of stitches on each row.

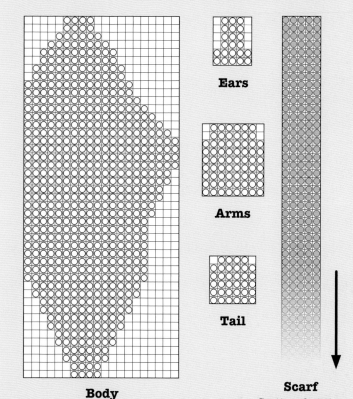

Ears

Arms

Tail

Body

Scarf

Continue knitting until you have 90 rows in total.

Feet

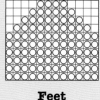

Liners

Liners are to scale.

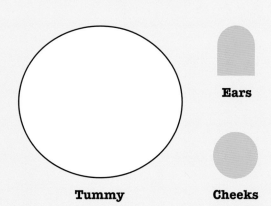

Tummy

Ears

Cheeks

17

9. Stuff the lower half of the body. When you are happy, sew up the hole at the bottom.

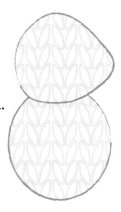

10. Sew the ears into place on the polar bear's head, as shown.

11. Sew the arms and feet onto the body, as shown. Your bear will need its feet to help it balance.

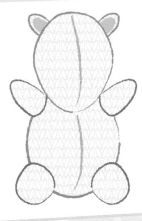

12. Sew the tail onto the bottom of the polar bear's body, as shown.

13. Using black embroidery thread, sew three large stitches onto the ends of the arms and feet, to give your bear claws.

14. Trace the tummy liner (page 17) onto white felt and cut out the shape. Pin it in place, then sew onto the tummy using a running stitch (page 9).

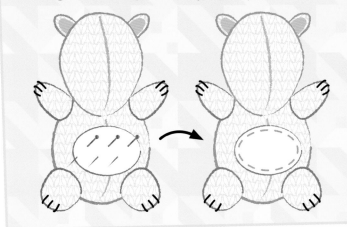

15. Trace the cheeks liner onto pink felt and cut out two pieces. Glue in place. Cut a black circle of felt for the nose and glue in place, or stitch on a button if you prefer. Then use black embroidery thread to carefully sew on a mouth.

16. Glue on black felt circles for the eyes, or stitch on buttons if you prefer.

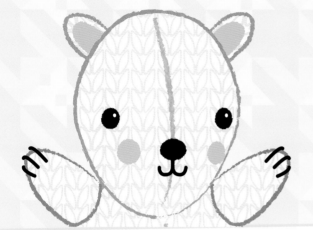

17. Use the scarf template (page 17) to knit a scarf in a color of your choice.

18. For the tassels, cut 12 strands of yarn roughly 4 in. long.

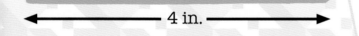

◄─────── 4 in. ───────►

19. Take two of the strands of yarn and place them together, as shown. Fold in half.

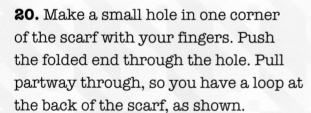

20. Make a small hole in one corner of the scarf with your fingers. Push the folded end through the hole. Pull partway through, so you have a loop at the back of the scarf, as shown.

21. Pull the ends of the strands through the loop and pull to tighten, as shown.

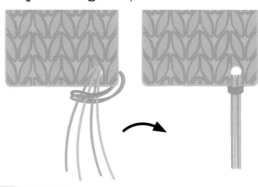

22. Repeat steps 19-21, adding two more tassels to the edge of your scarf.

23. Repeat steps 19-22 at the other end of the scarf. Sew in any loose ends of yarn, then wrap your bear up nice and cozy!

Top Tip

Add sequins and buttons to the scarf to make it look really cool!

Knitted Penguin

This little guy is super cute and loves a cuddle!

You will need:

- yarn in black and a color of your choice
- knitting needles • tracing paper
- felt or patterned fabric • pins
- needle and thread • stuffing
- scissors • fabric glue • a pompom
- two buttons, or black felt

2. Use the wings template opposite to knit two black wings.

3. Lay the two body pieces on top of each other. Place the straight ends of each wing between the body pieces, about halfway down, as shown. Pin all of the layers together.

1. First, use the body template opposite to knit two body pieces in black yarn.

4. Sew along the edge of the body pieces to secure the wings, as shown. Leave a small gap at the bottom where you can add stuffing.

5. Push stuffing into the penguin's body, making sure you push it up to the top with your fingers. When the body is full enough, sew up the hole at the bottom.

6. Trace the feet liner onto orange felt and cut out two pieces. Glue these into place on the bottom of the penguin. Sew in any loose ends of yarn.

Templates

Each dot represents the number of stitches on each row.

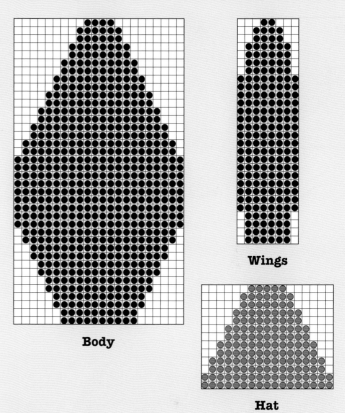

Body

Wings

Hat

Liners

Liners are to scale.

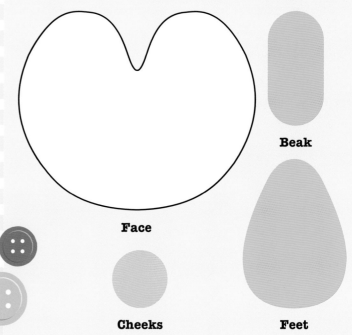

Face

Beak

Cheeks

Feet

7. Trace the face liner onto white felt and cut out the shape. Pin the face onto the penguin's head, then sew on using a running stitch (page 9).

8. Glue on black felt circles for the eyes, or stitch on buttons if you prefer. Trace the cheeks liner, cut out two pieces from pink felt, then glue in place.

9. Trace the beak liner onto orange felt and cut out the shape. Place it onto the face and stitch through the center to hold in place.

10. Using the hat template, knit two pieces in a color of your choice.

11. Place the two hat pieces on top of each other and pin together.

12. Sew along the top edges, leaving the bottom edge open, as shown. Sew in the ends of yarn to complete.

13. Glue a pompom on top of the hat. Now your penguin is ready to waddle off into the sunset!

Knitted Seal Pup

There is nothing sweeter than a seal pup—that's official!

You will need:

- gray yarn • knitting needles
- tracing paper • felt or patterned fabric
- pins • needle and thread • stuffing
- scissors • fabric glue
- three buttons, or black felt

1. First, use the body template (page 24) to knit two gray body pieces.

2. Lay the two body pieces on top of each other and pin them together.

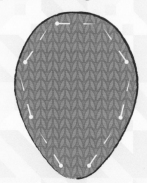

3. Sew along the edge of the body pieces, joining them together. Leave a small gap at the bottom where you can add stuffing.

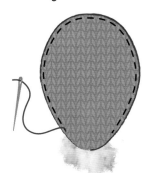

4. Push stuffing into the seal pup's body, making sure you push it up to the top with your fingers. When the body is full enough, sew up the hole at the bottom.

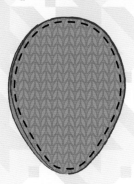

5. Use the flippers template (page 24) to knit two flippers from the same color yarn you used to make the body.

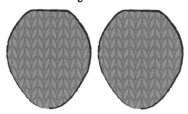

6. Sew these in place roughly halfway down the seal pup's body, as shown.

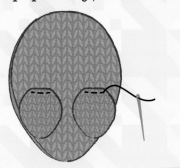

7. Using the tail template, knit a tail for your seal pup in the same color yarn you used for the body and flippers.

8. Place the tail at the back of the seal pup and sew in place with a few large stitches. Sew in any loose ends of yarn.

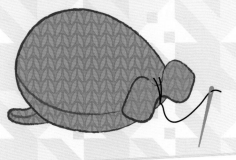

9. Glue on black felt circles for the eyes and nose, or stitch on buttons if you prefer.

10. Trace the cheeks liner. Cut out two pieces from pink felt, then glue in place. Finally, use black embroidery thread to carefully sew on a small mouth, as shown.

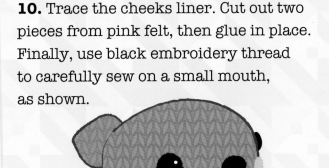

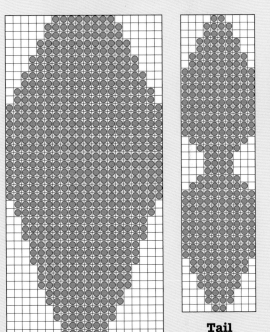

Templates

Each dot represents the number of stitches on each row.

Flippers

Tail

Body

Liner

Liner is to scale.

Cheeks